When Your Dad Goes to War:
Helping Children Cope with Deployment and Beyond

Maryann Makekau
with
20/30north Studios

Also available: When Your Mom Goes to War:
Helping Children Cope with Deployment and Beyond

Copyright 2010, 2020 by Makekau
Graphic Design: 20/3onorth Studios

All rights reserved. No part of this publication may be reproduced, stored in a retrieval system or transmitted, in any form or by any means, electronic, mechanical, photocopying, recording or otherwise, without the prior written permission of the author/publisher. Printed in the United States of America.

For information, address:
Hope Matters

PO Box 2021
Fort Walton Beach, FL 32549
contact@becausehopematters.com

Set in Kristen ITC 12 point. Includes references.

LITTLE PATRIOT BOOK™

When Your Dad Goes to War:
Helping Children Cope with Deployment and Beyond.

Library of Congress Cataloging (Pre-assigned Control Number)
Makekau, Maryann

ISBN-13: 978-0-9826601-8-8
ISBN-10: 0982660189

Note: The information in this book is true and complete to the best of our knowledge. This book is intended only as an informative guide for those wishing to know more about deployment issues. In no way is this book intended to replace, countermand or conflict with the advice given to you by other professionals, military authority, counselor or physician. The ultimate decision concerning care should be made between you, your family and professionals. We strongly recommend that you follow their advice. Information in this book is general and is offered with no guarantees on the part of the author or publisher. The author and publisher disclaim all liability in connection with use of this book.

In Memory of
WILLIS HENDERSON

Loving Husband, Gentle Father, Dedicated Soldier

FOREWORD

Deployments are pretty much a fact of life these days for most of those serving in the military. But it wasn't always that way. September 11, 2001, changed the world forever. I remember watching the live news video of the Twin Towers burning and thinking that life would never be the same again. Within 12 hours, I processed and loaded up with 150 Air Force medics to deploy to "somewhere" in what was the beginning of the Global War on Terror (GWOT).

Although that first trip was only to New Jersey for 10 days, the one that followed four days later took me to the Persian Gulf—the first of three deployments during the next four years. My family and I experienced many thoughts, emotions, and challenges as we prepared, embarked, and endured the months that followed. There was even the occasional thought of "Will we be together again?" During the next deployment, my wife and five children were left to endure a long North Dakota winter while I had an all-expenses paid trip to Iraq. My mission there was to help set up an EMEDS field hospital.

In the early days of the GWOT, nobody knew exactly how long deployments would last. It's difficult enough for an adult to cope with that uncertainty, but explaining it to children is even harder. How do you say, "Dad has to go away—to War—for a long time?" To a child, even two months can seem like a very long time. Six months or a year can seem like forever—just think of all the things that happen and the changes they go through in that time.

For some, deployments are planned months in advance. There is time to prepare for the changes in schedules, activities, and routines that everyone will face. Other families undergo abrupt changes as they face last minute deployments. Regardless of the timing, all families will likely encounter many events they cannot anticipate.

Dad has to train to do his job in another country with other troops so that the mission will be accomplished successfully. In the same way, the more training and preparation the family has, the more successful they will be, too. The ultimate goal is not simply to survive but to thrive during deployment and beyond.

Maryann's book offers practical advice and helpful resources for those left behind. Managing the separation productively will equip everyone to face similar and bigger challenges in the future. Applying the tips and resources in this book will help children and those caring for them—and dad—emerge from deployment with a stronger sense of self and family.

WAYNE SUMPTER
MD, Colonel USAF Retired

BRIEF COUNSEL

When your dad goes to war he leaves a vacuum in the family structure. During his deployment, children may experience fearful and emotional turbulence. Maryann Makekau vividly paints a portrait of a child's world when Dad's orders send him away from the family to serve his country. With insight, wisdom, humor, and faith, Maryann reframes this event by enjoining the children as valuable "team members." With sage words she encourages the children left behind in saying that "helping out makes you part of the journey."

Using whimsical drawings and language ease, she offers families various activities for each stage of deployment (preparation, separation, and re-unification). Even though Dad is not physically present, these creative activities INCLUDE dad, helping families maintain a sense of unity and wholeness.

With the help of their moms or caretakers, children can "take charge of their situation" in a productive way instead of feeling "left behind." Uncertainty and fear can be transformed into feelings of self-confidence and hope, providing a sense of mastery over events—which before reading this book may have seemed "uncontrollable."

These Little Patriot Books™ pack a powerful message that is full of valuable ideas, information, and resources. It is a "must-read" for every military family, extended families, educators, clergy, therapists, and others who interface regularly with military personnel and their children. Thank God for this valuable book!

CAROL MURPHY, LMHC, RN

St. Simon's Counseling Center
Fort Walton Beach Florida

DEDICATION

Whether writing about cancer, loss, grief, deployment or war, it's the child's experience that continues to capture my attention. Adults have an inherent responsibility to prepare children for tough times. Some subjects are so incomprehensible though, that it may be tempting to avoid such conversations.

Yet, being forthright allows for honest communication within the family. Those talks must be delivered in a way that children can understand, spoken on their terms. Otherwise, children tend to simply follow adults rather than express themselves.

Just as I created the Little Pink Book™ series to help families cope with cancer, it is my desire to bring similar hope and understanding to families coping with deployment through these Little Patriot Books.™

This book is dedicated to the troops who voluntarily serve and protect our freedoms, and to their selfless families who also sacrifice so much. My active duty service followed by years as a career military spouse raising two "brats" amidst my career in mental health sculpted this opportunity to give back. When Your Dad Goes to War and When Your Mom Goes to War are my way of blessing military families engaged in the war on terror.

I'm grateful for the numerous interviews with the troops and their families, and also thank all the military organizations and advocates who opened their doors and their hearts to help me gain crucial insight. A special note of thanks to: Willis, Tina, Jason, Andrea, Deidre, Donald, Erica, Al, Melinda, Alan, Erin, Christopher, Natalie, Krissy and Mary.

Thank you to my husband Chuck, my family, friends, foreword writers and endorsers for contributing to my work. Thank you to my editor, Amaryllis Sánchez Wohlever, MD for tireless reviews. Thanks to my artist Derek, for the gifts you bring to my life and to these Little Patriot Books™. God bless our soldiers for the freedoms we have due to their sacrifices—may we never forget.

TABLE OF CONTENTS

1 – OPERATION DESERT-BOUND

2 – MAPPING IT OUT

3 – SEE YOU LATER

4 – RED WHITE AND BLUE AND FEELINGS IN BETWEEN

5 – THE WORRY BOX

6 – STAYING THE COURSE

7 – JUST LIKE YOU DAD

8 – PATRIOT'S CODE OF CONDUCT

9 – OPERATION HOMEBOUND

10 - LITTLE PATRIOT'S CHECKLIST

TIPS FOR FAMILIES
TIPS FOR EDUCATORS
HELPFUL RESOURCES AND LINKS
JOURNAL

OPERATION DESERT-BOUND

Soldiers in the military are like a really, really big family—bigger than anyone's family you've ever met. Some soldiers are in the branch called the Army and some are in the Air Force. Some are in the branch called the Marines and some are in the Navy. And still others are in the branches called Reserves, National Guard, or Coast Guard.

It's hard to imagine a family that big; it's sort of like looking at a huge Sequoia tree. It can stand hundreds of feet tall and have lots of strong branches that connect to one giant trunk! The branches all grow together by being part of that huge tree. When the branches of the military come together like that, they can make a big difference in a war or anywhere that they go.

Soldiers can be very strong with tools like armored tanks, bombers, fighter planes, carriers, chem-gear, and combat boots! It can get confusing to hear words like deployments, rotations, sorties, Afghanistan, soldiers, insurgents, platoon, ranger, airman, and captain. Deployment means that your dad has to go to work away from the family, usually in a place that's far from home. Watching your dad prepare for deployment can feel like your house has turned upside down. All of a sudden, your dad has lots of things to do and places to go. There's lots of gear to pack, and his deployment checklist is longer than any homework assignment you've ever seen! He needs to be fit for duty and ready to go, and getting there can feel like a huge event.

Although you can't go with your dad on his deployment, helping out makes you part of the journey! You might have so many questions that you don't know how to even ask them. Ask your dad how you can help him. Maybe you can help him put together his 72-hour bag, which your dad will carry with him at all times. Whatever you do to help, things get done faster with team effort!

Some kids have to change houses and other kids get to stay right where they are. Whether you're staying in your own home during your dad's deployment or going someplace else, you can take your dad's love with you because that's always in your heart. Your dad will make sure that someone is there to take care of you no matter where you stay while he's away.

Getting together with other kids whose mom or dad is deployed can be a big help. You can share stories, ideas, feelings and more!

MAPPING IT OUT

Having all hands on deck means that everyone comes together to help—before, during, and after your dad's deployment. Staying connected as a family is really important. Even though you can't go with your dad, you can be part of his deployment in lots of different ways!

You can talk to your dad about his gear—ask questions about how it's used in the war zone and ask if you can try on a few things, too. You can't be the "man of the house" or take dad's place, but you can try on his shoes! Just wearing his shoes shows you that you have lots of growing to do, but it's fun to pretend to be just like dad. It's important to ask first, though, because your dad's chem-gear, combat boots, dog tags, and fleece are all really, really important desert gear.

You can take your imagination on Google with the help of an adult. You type in an address on the Internet and Google Earth takes you there! You can travel to where your dad's going, to a friend's house or to your grandparents' place or anywhere else you want to explore. It's a virtual ride on your computer! Did you know that there are many other nations supporting the war effort, too? Google places like the Netherlands, Canada, Italy, Germany, Afghanistan, and more!

Sometimes there are special events just for kids whose parents are deploying. You might get to try on other kinds of gear and go inside airplanes, ships or tanks. You might even get your own deployment checklist and supplies to take home! This book has a "Little Patriot's Checklist" to help you find your place in the ranks of helping, too!

Mapping it out helps families before deployment and all the way through it. You don't have to miss out during your dad's deployment; collect some things that will help you along the way. A wipe-off board helps everyone in the family make "happening notes." Those are things that happen between phone calls and letters—and writing them down makes it easy to remember when it's time to share again. Keep a stack of paper and crayons in the kitchen for refrigerator art; then you can be ready to create amazing pictures for dad whenever you have free time! Just hang a picture-of-the-week on the fridge until it's mail or phone time.

SEE YOU LATER

Saying good bye can be easy to do when you're going to play with a friend or leaving for a day at school. But saying good bye when it's for a much longer time is not the same thing at all. It seems like no matter how much you prepare for it, actually doing it is different than you thought.

Whether you've thought it over in your mind or chose not to think about it at all, when it's time for your dad to deploy, you'll have to say "see you later." You've got dad's love in your heart, you've helped him pack and you've done a virtual tour of where he's going, but you still might not be ready to say good bye.

Being apart is a big deal for everyone in the family. You can practice ahead of time by hugging often, drawing pictures for your dad and taking on new chores before he leaves. Sometimes, practicing makes things easier. It's sort of like practicing before a baseball game; you're more ready for the game when you already know how to play.

Even though saying good bye isn't fun like playing a game, it's still something you have to do. Sometimes good byes bring lots of tears, hugs and kisses or saying special things like "I love you" and "see you later." But sometimes good byes are filled with silence—it's like no one knows quite what to say. Any of those good byes are okay. Just make sure you don't miss out on saying, "see you later alligator!"

RED WHITE AND BLUE AND FEELINGS IN BETWEEN

Feelings are like the colors of the rainbow because there are some that are really bright and bold while others are hard to see. Red is one of those colors that really get your attention, like a fire hydrant or a stop sign. Have you ever been so mad that you "see red?" That's one of those adult sayings. It's like when you work super hard on your homework and then you lose it before school! It gets you so mad that you see red!

Adults get mad and frustrated about things too, and they feel red just like kids do sometimes. It's okay if you get really mad at times as long as you don't stay that way. It's no fun to be around somebody who's mad all the time.

happy   sad   angry

Have you ever heard an adult say that they're "blue?" Blue is one of those feelings that are a little harder to see and can be even harder to talk about. It's that feeling when everything seems to go wrong or when your best friend moves away, when you feel like crying. Having your dad deploy might make you red-faced mad or blue-faced sad or even scared.

Scared is a dark color, a feeling that something bad will happen, or how you feel when you wake up suddenly from a bad dream. You try to go back to sleep, but all you can think about is your bad dream. Climbing out of bed for some milk and cookies or snuggling with someone safe can give you good thoughts and help you get back to sleep.

Calm is like the color white, like when you're playing quietly or reading a good book. Pink is a good color for smiling and purple is for riding your bike, and perhaps you're feeling yellow when you add a new ribbon on the map!

Talk about all of your feelings whether you're happy, scared, angry, sad, frustrated or confused! If you're feeling red, white or blue or somewhere in between, it's very important to share your feelings with others. You can talk about your feelings and you can even draw them. Just draw your face, add your color, and tape it on your bedroom door—then everyone in your family will know exactly how you're feeling, especially on tough days.

scared

frustrated

confused

It's always important to let your feelings out so that you can feel better and move on with other stuff, like playing and having fun! Write down some of your feelings to share with dad because talking on the phone or Skyping might be really short.

Skyping is sort of like being on television but you get to hear and see each other! You can also write letters, make cards, draw pictures, and talk on the telephone. Deployed parents get homesick too, so talking to you and getting mail from you will really help your dad a lot!

THE WORRY BOX

Some feelings can be really hard to put into words. It's good to share your feelings, though, including the things you worry about—whether you're feeling red, white or blue or somewhere in between! Not sharing your worries might make you feel sad, have bad dreams, get stomach aches or even have trouble doing your school work. Letting go of your worries gives you more time to do other stuff, like playing outside with your friends.

Sometimes kids have really big worries like "what if my dad gets hurt or dies?" You're not alone because adults have big worries like that too.

If your mom is in charge, she may be scared and confused about having to handle everything without your dad. If dad was the one who took care of the lawn, car and home repairs, or helped with after-school activities—that's a lot of stuff for your mom to do. Helping each other and letting other people help your family means everyone worries less about everything!

An old shoe box can be recycled and used to make a "Worry Box." When you're worried or scared, just drop a note or picture in your Worry Box. You can write favorite words on it; draw pictures or add your favorite colors. You might say a simple prayer as you drop it in—like "God bless my dad!"

When it's really quiet you might miss your dad even more, like when you're sitting in your room or in church. Turn your worries into hope by thanking God for your dad. Thinking about good things will take your mind off of all the things you're worried about.

Even though your dad is your hero whether he's at war or home, you'll have to share him for a while. He might be on the front lines protecting people, building a road or bridge, or helping women and children learn to read or get medical help. He might be loading planes with supplies or carrying special equipment on a really big ship into the war zone. He might be providing all the meals to the soldiers who are deployed. By doing those things, soldiers are everyone's hero.

STAYING THE COURSE

Change can be hard, but making changes can also teach you some very important things. You discover new things when you learn to be flexible and see change as part of life. You learn that when you move and say goodbye to friends, your family is still there with you! You learn that you can make it through hard times and even enjoy some new things along the way!

When something isn't easy, it can be really hard to keep going. If you're having a hard time reading books or doing Math, perhaps you've thought about quitting. If you've had a hard time learning to ride your bike you might be tempted to quit when you fall down.

Instead, you can work even harder than you ever have before! Staying the course means that you won't quit! No matter how hard it is to wait and wait some more for your dad to come home, you'll stay the course. So if you promised to practice bike riding or working on Math or Reading, you keep trying! Slowly, what seemed impossible now seems possible. What was once scary isn't so scary anymore. Everything looks different when you conquer your fears! You'll feel braver and smarter—it's like you've won a prize!

One of the hardest things about missing your dad is not having him around for important dates, like holidays and birthdays. You can take lots of pictures and share them on Skype (which let's you see and hear your dad) or on the phone even though it won't be exactly like having your dad around. You can ask for rain-checks for holidays and birthdays that your dad misses. Rain-checks are like saying it is okay to have it later. You might even celebrate everything in one day, all at once, when your dad comes home. You can get birthday party hats, have a turkey for dinner and open presents wrapped in Christmas paper!

If your dad misses your birthday, you can mark DFK on the

calendar for dad's return. DFK stands for "Dad for Kid" day, and that means it will be just you and your dad—together you decide where you'll go and what you'll do! Maybe your DFK is about shooting some hoops, going fishing or seeing a new movie. Finding new ways to do things together means that you and your dad don't have to miss out just because you have to wait! Using your imagination can be lots of fun and it sure makes staying the course through deployment easier for everyone!

JUST LIKE YOU DAD

Your dad isn't like any other dad. Maybe he builds awesome LEGO forts, shoots amazing baskets in the backyard or tells funny jokes while you're fishing together. Your dad might be really good at setting up a tent and roasting marshmallows!

Although you can't do all of those things, you can do some things like dad does. You can sit in his favorite chair while watching television! You can build a tent in your room using bed sheets! Bring a flashlight in your tent and read a book, like this one!

You can still shoot hoops in the backyard and you might even keep score so you can tell your dad when he calls! You can make a LEGO city like the one where your dad's staying using LEGO helmets, jeeps, Army men and tents! If you live near a military station, you can go eat at the chow hall just like dad. The chow hall (or mess hall) is the place where soldiers eat, and sometimes kids and their families get to eat there, too. Your dad might be sitting down to eat far from home but he'll be thinking of you, eating in the same kind of place. By doing some of the things that your dad does, you'll feel closer to him even though you're far apart.

When you go shopping you can look for pajamas, shirts, hats or backpacks in camouflaged colors. Dressing up and pretending to be just like dad can be lots of fun. You might find a place that makes "dog tags." Have them engraved with your dad's name and keep them near your bed so you remember to pray for him. Praying for your dad while he's at war can help you sleep better by letting go of all your worries. Your prayers will help him, too! Remember your Worry Box? You can put your prayers in there too!

You can learn about things that your dad is seeing while deployed. Ask your teacher to help your class learn about places like Iraq and Afghanistan. What's the weather like there? What kind of plants grow there and what do they look like? Are there any wild animals? Maybe your class can do a special project to learn all those things! Maybe you can fill up a poster with things you discover by using the Internet with an adult or visiting your library or a bookstore.

LITTLE PATRIOT'S CODE OF CONDUCT

You can have a patriotic attitude, just like real soldiers. You can show respect for other people by saying please and thank you. You can have integrity; that means doing what's right even when no one's looking—no shortcuts or excuses—like making time to study for your Spelling test so you get a good grade. Respect and integrity are part of the Little Patriot's Code of Conduct!

Helping is a way of doing excellent things. It's like a gift that gives twice. You feel good about helping and the person getting help feels really good too! Helping others can get you through a tough time; it takes your mind off of your worries and gets you thinking about other people.

Neighbors and friends like to be helpful when a parent's deployed. They might take turns mowing the lawn, raking the yard or shoveling snow. It's easier for people to help when you make a list of things to do! If you write the helper's name next to what they helped with, you can show it to dad when he gets home. It can take lots of people to do all of the dad kind-of-stuff!

You can look up all of the holidays that celebrate the troops: July 4th, Veterans Day, Memorial Day, Patriot's Day, and more! Then brainstorm about how to celebrate those days. You might get permission to hand out yellow ribbons for people to put on their mailboxes. You can talk to your teacher about having a "Hooah card day"—a day that says the military is totally awesome. All the students in your class can make cards for the troops. You might talk to your family, a youth leader or a teacher about recognizing your dad or saying a special prayer that day!

If you live near a military station, there might be special days there filled with fun things to do for kids of deployed parents. If not, get an adult's help to create some special things at your church, school, kids club, bowling center or even a water park. Maybe you can help create a "Patriot's Pride Day" just for kids whose parents are deployed!

There are lots of ways to show your patriotic pride—the sky's the limit! Giving back and helping others lets you see that you're not alone and there are other kids missing their deployed dad or mom, too.

OPERATION HOMEBOUND

Some deployments last less than a month while others last months and months. No matter how long you've waited it might feel like forever. Then, that time finally comes—dad is coming home!

Now that he's on the way, you might feel butterflies in your stomach—that nervous feeling on the inside, that's almost like when you get really, really hungry. It's normal for kids to feel nervous and excited, especially when you haven't seen your dad for a long time.

You might have a million questions. What if he's changed and he's not like you remember? What if you've changed and he doesn't recognize you? What if he doesn't like the way you've changed your room or the new style of clothes you're wearing? Will he still like you?

Of course he still likes you! He loves you and can't wait to see you too! So put all those worries in your worry box. Just like your family pulled together before deployment, you can all pull together after deployment and beyond. Everyone changes some as they get older and when they go through new things in life. So you and your dad will be different in some ways, but the love you share will never change!

Even when you misbehave, your dad still loves you. Even when you break something by accident, he still loves you. He loves you no matter how long he's away. He loves you from half-way across the world!

Hugging is a really important way to show your love. Hugging someone you haven't seen in a long time can be sort of tricky. If you've grown up a lot during your dad's deployment, hugging might feel different than you remember. Hugging feels different as you grow taller! You might not remember exactly how your dad sounds or smells, and that makes it feel different. It's okay to take it slow. Maybe you go with the 2-second hug until you're ready for the bear-hug. Or you go with the one-armed hug until you're ready for the big squeeze.

For a lot of families, this is the hardest part of deployment. Your family might have done things a little differently while dad was deployed. Doing things differently isn't wrong—it's just different!

Remember how at home and at school you have to take turns? Taking turns gives everyone a chance to be part of doing things. Even parents can take turns. They can take turns making decisions. They can take turns doing the chores and driving kids places. Taking turns means everyone is included, no matter how they do things. Different is okay as long as everybody's safe and stuff gets done!

Living with other soldiers for a long time is different than living at home. Living with a bunch of guys is very different than living with a daughter or son, and different than living with a wife. So you might have to refresh your dad—give him some time to catch up and get used to things at home again.

It might take everyone a while to catch up and feel like part of the crew again. Being part of the crew is like having your place in the ranks—everybody's place in a family is important; everybody gives different gifts. Your gifts are what you give to your family just by sharing your ideas, your help, and your love. Welcome your dad back and enjoy all those things that make your family unique!

LITTLE PATRIOT'S CHECKLIST

1. Remember that your dad deployed because it's his job. Nothing you did or didn't do caused him to leave to fight in the war.

2. Helping your family is one of the most important jobs in the world.

3. Hug others until they let go first; it's really fun to see how long a hug lasts!

4. Crying is like cleaning your body from the inside out—everyone needs cleaning like that sometimes. Be ready with hugs when this happens at your house—and let others know when you need one yourself!

5. Take your Patriot attitude to other places like school, sporting events and church. Your attitude of respect and integrity will encourage others to do excellent things too!

6. Share your feelings—happy, sad, angry, mad, frustrated or confused. Families are stronger when they can share all those important feelings with each other.

7. Have fun. Play often. Laugh a lot. Use your imagination. Explore the outdoors. Eat well. Stay strong. Love others. Pray for the troops.

8. As a Little Patriot, you serve our nation, too. Remind your friends to be thankful for our troops, their families, and freedom!

TIPS FOR FAMILIES

1. Forgetting some things over time is normal. To help your child remember dad during deployment, make time to look at photos, talk about good times, and talk on the phone or Skype. Even brief moments of sharing help keep memories intact.

2. Encourage each other to flow with the changes brought on by deployment. Change is an inevitable part of life, although some take longer to adapt than others. Resist the tendency to compare and always celebrate individual milestones.

3. Create a convoy of helps. Asking for help is a sign of strength; it means you know your own limits. Make a list of things dad usually does so that when others ask to help, you can simply let them choose from the list.

4. Have a practice run. If dad gets advanced deployment notice, start using some of the tips in this book and others your family creates. It will allow dad to focus on preparing for deployment and help the family to adjust to things being different, even before he departs.

5. If possible, meet with the principal and school teachers prior to dad's departure. Explain how deployment will affect your family and share some your family's needs—from watching your child for signs of distress to understanding absences and more.

6. Engage children as much as possible in the deployment journey: helping dad pack, mailing treats, having two kitchen clocks for each time zone and creating a welcome home banner. Keep activities age-appropriate and minimize media coverage that may be biased or too graphic.

7. If your child is withdrawing, crying frequently, becoming aggressive or showing other problem behaviors be supportive and understanding. Reach out for professional help if you don't see signs of improvement.

TIPS FOR FAMILIES (CONT.)

8. Pass it on. If dad has gone to war before, share what you've learned with families new to deployment. Also share important things you've learned with teachers, church staff, coaches, friends, and relatives—anyone who frequently spends time with your child.

9. If a mentor is involved during deployment, help your child transition afterwards so that they won't feel conflicted about sharing time with dad and their mentor.

10. Worrying isn't a job—you don't get paid for it! Avoid spending time worrying about what hasn't happened and what you can't control. Pray and let go; spend time everyday being thankful.

TIPS FOR EDUCATORS

1. Be aware that the vast majority of military children don't live on military installations; they are an integral part of civilian communities. They don't stand out like their parent(s) in uniform.

2. Keep in mind that some children stay behind with a non-deployed parent, while others live temporarily with a relative or family friend. Some children even have to relocate during a parent's deployment—thrusting them into different homes, classrooms and communities.

3. If a new student shows up at school, ask questions and give extra support perhaps through a buddy arrangement, follow up phone calls and caregiver-teacher meetings.

4. Arrange extra support for any child whose parent is deployed, whether or not the child has relocated, and no matter how many times a parent deploys—every deployment is difficult.

5. Encourage other students to show support for parents' military service; involve the classroom in letter-writing and card-making campaigns for the troops.

6. Invite returning troops into their child's classroom. Encourage them to share age-appropriate parts of the deployment journey so that other students can identify with a soldier's lifestyle and sacrifices too.

7. Be watchful for tearfulness, anxiety, acting out, comments or drawings that are worrisome or other problem behaviors that may indicate an emotional toll from parental absence.

8. Be mindful of political views, news stories, and areas of study; honor the troops (student's parents) by monitoring what is shared in the classroom.

9. Encourage patriotic pride by engaging students in marked calendar events that honor our nation and our troops.

10. Consider arranging a small support group with the school counselor for students whose parents are deployed—giving them an opportunity to share with others who are going through the same things.

HELPFUL RESOURCES AND LINKS

References used in this publication:

- Military Officer Magazine, April 2010, "War Hits Home" article by Ellen N. Woods.
- http://www.military.com/benefits/resources/deployment/your-children-and-separation
- www.MilitaryOneSource.com
- http://www.airforcetimes.com/family/military_kidstress_tips_070904w/

Other Helpful Resources and Links:

- Hearts Apart Programs
- Airman and Family Support Center
- Army Community Services
- Fleet and Family Services

JOURNAL

JOURNAL